The
Emotional
Rehabilitation of
Valentino

Vicky Flora

iUniverse

THE EMOTIONAL REHABILITATION OF VALENTINO

iUniverse books may be ordered through booksellers or by contacting:

iUniverse
1663 Liberty Drive
Bloomington, IN 47403
www.iuniverse.com
1-800-Authors (1-800-288-4677)

ISBN: 978-1-5320-1115-3 (sc)
ISBN: 978-1-5320-1114-6 (e)

Library of Congress Control Number: 2016918683

Print information available on the last page.

iUniverse rev. date: 11/16/2016

To Dr. Dale A. Flora, my husband, my friend, my love

Acknowledgments

A special thank-you to Kathryn Barnum for the cover artwork; Kate is not only a phenomenal artist but a compassionate human being who gives her time as a hospice volunteer. Thank you, Kate; I am amazed at your ability to capture the look of Valentino as you have.

Thank you to Misty Vee, a fellow respiratory therapist, for her proofreading.

Thank you to my husband for his support in this endeavor. You know of my need to give Valentino a loving home. You have been there with love and support for him always.

Thank you to Shannon Zariski for not only being the best daughter a mother could have but being the corporate secretary a clinical person like myself needs.

Thank you to Robert Zariski for the work on the pictures. Robert, you were able to take simple pictures from my phone and make them print ready.

Introduction

I am a person who has enjoyed having a pet in my home for my entire life. I have had several cats, dogs, fish, horses, and a hamster, but I have never had an animal that has touched my heart the first time I saw him, the way Valentino did. The picture I'd seen of him on the Internet had shown a white dog, his hair shaved short and his head hanging as if he was giving up on life. He was a small dog in a cage, and under his picture was "Valentino: Bichon Frise." I had to see him and if possible bring him to a home he could become comfortable in.

Within the first few days of bringing Valentino home, I decided I would document his behavior and the different things he did, or that I did to get a response from him, because I had never had an animal so visibly and physically frightened. I wondered what others had done in this situation.

I am aware of animal therapists, but I am also aware that not everyone can afford therapy for his or her animals. The pet therapist at the store came over to us while we were talking to the foster home caregivers and offered me her card. She stated that an animal showing as much fear as Valentino did would need work and that she would like to have therapy sessions with him. I don't know why, but I didn't want someone else to work with him. I wanted to do it myself. I think I just wanted to show this frightened animal that he could trust me.

Many people may not be aware that their animals needs more than food, water, and a warm bed. In the case of Valentino, the need was for time, patience, a sense of safety, and acceptance. It is the same with raising children, and it is possible that the empty-nest mother in me came out. We also have a Brittany named Chase, who is a very loving dog, and I felt he would help give Valentino companionship different from what a human can give. Whatever the reason behind my decision, I was determined to adopt this dog.

This is our story.

February 19, 2012

Dale, my husband, and I picked up Valentino from a rescue. When we removed him from the carrier, he crouched next to the wall and trembled. He would not make eye contact. I knelt by him and put a hand on his back. Not only could I feel his tremors, but I could see them. The foster lady had explained that many people had asked to see him because he was a bichon frise, but no one had taken him because, in her words, he "did not show well."

My first thought was that he did not have to "show well." He just needed to be a safe animal that I could trust if one of my grandchildren came near him. It didn't take long for me to see that Valentino was nonaggressive. He didn't growl, show his teeth, or give any sign that he would be a danger to anyone.

I held him during the ride home, but he turned away from me if I tried to look at his cute face. Once home, he hid under the high chair in the dining room. Sometimes he would move to another area if anyone came close to him, always under something like a table or chair. At other times he would cower and turn his head away yet allow me to touch him.

This was his first day in our home, and I started what I call "holding therapy" to work on building trust and giving love. I carried him to the living room and sat on the couch with him on my lap for about an hour. During this time he stopped trembling but remained tense, still refusing eye contact. I continued the holding therapy daily for the first few weeks that we had him. I wanted to see if he would get used to being touched without being afraid. He did improve and stopped trembling after the first couple of minutes, but he still would not look at me. I would try to look at his cute face, but he would turn his head away.

We caught him raising a leg on the dining room table, and the yell out of Dale ended that in a hurry. Valentino will be given love, but he will also have direction as to what is or is not acceptable behavior.

He came into our bedroom during the night. I think I was only half sleeping when he entered, but I was alert to any need he had, so I got up and took him outside. After several minutes, he still would not let me pick him up to return to the house. Every time I got close, he ran away. It was twelve degrees outside, and we were both very cold. After several laps around the fenced-in yard, he finally gave in and let me pick him up. I think we will use his leash tomorrow night.

February 20, 2012

When we got up in the morning, Valentino was still under the high chair, but he had one of Chase's rawhide chews with him. It was a good sign that he had been out exploring. He ate about one third of his breakfast and still remained elusive. He was easy to pick up, and I put his sweater on for his day in the kennel. His food, water, and a heater supplied his needs for the day, and I had high hopes that he would bond more with Chase, as they would be in the kennel together.

We have what I think is a pretty good setup for the dogs when we leave. There is an indoor kennel in the garage, with a doggy door going out to a large kennel outside. The outdoor kennel has a gate going into the backyard, and we keep the gate open most of the time. This gives the dogs a large run area and the ability to look in through the patio door when we get home. It also makes it very easy for us to let them in and out as needed.

When I returned from work, I found that he had one arm out of his sweater, and he was not as eager to see me as Chase was. With Chase jumping at the kennel door to greet me, Valentino was trying to go out the doggy door of their kennel, but his little legs were too short. He got his front paws up and his head out, but his little white butt was popping up without getting the height needed to get him out the door. Sad as it was, it was the first time he made me laugh. We will create a ramp or steps for him tonight.

The evasive behavior continued through the evening, but the holding therapy showed improvement. After the first few minutes, he not only quit shaking, but he relaxed and laid his head on my arm. He might even have gone to sleep. It was hard to tell.

During the night, Chase woke Dale for potty time. It was a little late, as there was stool in the hallway from both Valentino and Chase. Only Chase would have asked to go out at that time, but it was not like him to mess in the house. It is our guess that Chase was not going to let Valentino mark territory that he thought was his.

Later in the night, Valentino let out his first bark, which got me up for potty time. I thought I was smart to use the leash this time, but he would not walk with the leash. He stood in one place as if he was frozen already. I finally put the leash down, but nothing changed. I went into the house, thinking that if I left him alone for a few minutes, he would do his job.

As I continued to watch him through the patio door, it was plain to see that he was not going to move for quite some time, so I disconnected the leash. Still nothing changed. He may have been too cold to move by that time; I know I was.

I went back in to get some sleep and start over tomorrow.

February 21, 2012

When we got up, Valentino was still under the high chair, and he continued to monitor my movements as I prepared breakfast. He ate very little. After eating I opened the patio door, and Chase went out. After a few evasive moves to avoid walking by me, Valentino followed.

When Chase came in, I began to panic. I could not find Valentino. I could see the entire fenced-in yard, and I looked in the kennel in the garage—and still no Valentino. I went into the house and dressed for the hunt in the cold, praying that he hadn't gotten out into the road. I started with a review of the yard and kennel.

I found him in the doghouse in the outside kennel. No other dog we've had has ever liked that house. He did not seem surprised or afraid that I'd found him. Maybe he is getting used to the fact that I will be there checking on him. We will fill the doghouse with straw or leftover hay for him tonight. I put the remaining food in the kennel, the same as yesterday. Valentino allowed me to pick him up and carry him to the kennel.

I've noticed that he doesn't look away as much when he notices me looking at him. I think we are making progress.

In the evening he walked around the house more than he has since joining our family, but those little legs can sure move in the opposite direction if he finds he has walked into our path.

Dale brought home a kennel cage for Valentino to sleep in. I think he likes it. We leave the door open, and he goes into it to lie down. We thought that if this dog had spent a lot of time in a kennel in his short life of three years, he may feel comfort in the confinement.

I did take him from his kennel and held him on my lap for over an hour again. This time he relaxed and slept in my arms. I hope he enjoyed that as much as I did.

February 22, 2012

Wow! Last night was the first night I got to sleep without getting up to take care of Valentino. I really needed the sleep. I feel like we have a new baby in the house. I served the dogs breakfast, with Chase eating in his usual place in the kitchen. I opened the door of Valentino's kennel and placed his dish just outside for him. This seemed to work well.

After they both ate less than half of what I'd given them, Chase wanted to go out, and Valentino pranced out behind him. He did not seem upset him that I was standing there. That is progress.

My joy was short-lived, lasting only until I wanted to put Valentino's coat on for his day in the garage kennel and yard. We did several laps around the circle that is the path from the dining room, through the living room, through the kitchen, and back into the dining room. He finally went into his kennel, and I was able to dress him for his day outside and in the garage kennel. It was not easy dressing him while I was on my hands and knees, half in the kennel myself. I'm not sure a sweater is necessary for him. It may be too much work for me and anxiety for him.

He still moves evasively if we enter the room he is in, and several times he has left his kennel cage if I walked too close to it. He went out the patio door with Chase, but he went from the backyard to the outside kennel and then into the garage kennel. Only when we went into the garage did he go back the other way and enter the house through the open patio door. Several times we played this little game of cat and mouse, so to speak.

At one point, I lay down in front of the open kennel cage door and softly talked to him as he lay resting. I lightly petted him, and he trembled for the first few seconds. After he relaxed, I placed a few treats by him and left.

February 25, 2012

I want to learn more about the bichon frise breed—mainly what their personality type is like when they are not emotionally stunted like Valentino. I found a book titled simply *Bichon Frise* by Martin Weil. This book covers everything on the bichon: history, breeding, grooming, and a chapter titled "Personality and Temperament." This chapter tells of a breed that is "confident, intelligent, highly attentive and who greatly enjoys the comfort, company, and love of the people who will comprise his family" (M. Weil 1981).

The more I read, the more I found clues as to what Valentino needed but hadn't received, being from a "puppy mill." The book stated that the puppy, "to be fostered to his full temperamental growth, should be cuddled often." Also, "without such displays of affection, the pup may become shy and withdrawn, without much human contact the true personality of the Bichon may never blossom" (M. Weil 1981).

Wow! This explained a lot of what we were seeing in Valentino. I'm willing to bet that Valentino was never cuddled—or shown love at all, for that matter. The only information we had received on Valentino before the adoption was that he had been rescued from a puppy mill.

I am even more determined to show this sweet dog that he will have love and safety in our home.

March 20, 2012

Today was Valentino's first grooming appointment. With all our walks in the yard at night, I have him leash trained now. He holds very still while I connect the leash to his collar, and then he is ready to walk.

His groomer's name is Rhonda, and I have decided I will book all of his appointments with her as long as she is available. My reasoning for this is the lack of trust Valentino has with people, and the fewer people he has to deal with, the easier it will be on him. He will have a chance to become comfortable with Rhonda, and maybe he will even trust her.

After being groomed, Valentino was even more adorable. Rhonda stated that he was quite easy to work with because he was so scared he didn't move. He would crouch down, and she would put her hand under his belly to bring him back to standing. That little dance went on until he was groomed and glowing white. He came right up to me when I arrived to get him. That gave me hope that he knows he is my dog, and that's okay with him.

I thought it would be good to keep Valentino with the same groomer for each visit because of his fear of strangers. Having the same groomer each time, he might develop trust in her. But Rhonda will be off work for a while, and Jessica will take his next appointments. I think when you have a dog as nervous as Valentino, having a professional groomer is best. They have dealt with many animal situations, making their training and experience valuable.

July 16, 2013

Valentino does not seem to need the kennel for protection as much as he did when we first brought him home. He seems just as comfortable sleeping on the floor in the living room. This is a huge step, showing that he feels safe sleeping in other rooms in the open where people walk, sit, and even talk to him without his heading for the safety of his kennel. If he feels safe in every room of our home, we are doing something right. I still don't want to move the kennel; he needs a safe zone.

August 19, 2013

What a change six months has made! Valentino now gets into a playful mood and takes off as fast as he can, running the circle through living room, dining room, kitchen, and hall. At times he will break the circle to run down the hall, slide on the bathroom rug, and come back as fast as his little legs will carry him. It is so funny to watch him. You just need to stay out of his way and enjoy his acting like he is having the time of his life.

He has also found his voice. He will bark at cats walking out by the barn when we are home, and when we are at the cottage, any stray dog is quickly told to get out of his yard. Both Chase and Valentino spend much of their time on the closed-in deck when we are at the lake. A baby gate has worked well.

As for his comfort zone, he only seems to be scared when I take him to the groomer. I think if Chase went too it would help, but Dale does the grooming on Chase.

Valentino does not have a problem getting into the truck when we go up north, as long as Chase gets into the truck first. When we are up north, Valentino still sleeps in a kennel we have there. I think he likes to hide there because that is the residence where we have the most company. People come to the lake and sometimes bring their dogs.

The only other dog Valentino likes is Chase, and I think the feeling is mutual. They are best friends. Having no fenced yard at the cottage, we walk the dogs twice a day. Valentino seems to enjoy the walks. At first he stayed close to Chase and did not want Chase to get ahead of him. How he takes his time and has to sniff out every new scent he finds, letting Dale and Chase get past curves in the road so he loses sight of them. After spending so much of his first three years in a cage, there is much that is new to him, and I think he enjoys the discovery.

Valentino now has a very good appetite. I take this as a sign that he is now fully comfortable in our home. I can hold him without his trembling, even if he still doesn't like to be looked in the face when I am close to him. He doesn't mind being looked at if I'm far enough away that I can't pick him up, but once I have him in my arms, he doesn't want eye contact.

He only goes into his kennel if we have other people over. His lack of trust in humans is probably going to be with him forever. I look at all these points and take pride that he is behaving as one of our family, which is good enough for me. He does not have to trust or like others.

November 26, 2013

We have a new addition to the family: a small kitten Dale found outside his office and rescued from the bitter cold winter we are having. The little thing had run across the road the night before as if returning to one of the houses there, but he was back in the bushes by Dale's office door again in the morning.

He was so small that I thought I would need to protect him from Chase and Valentino's being rough with him, but we have nothing to worry about. He is more aggressive in playing with them than they are with him. I think Valentino likes him, because he will not move if the kitten comes up to him or takes a nap by him. I have named the kitten Mr. Boots because of his four white feet.

February 19, 2014

I cannot believe it has been two years since we adopted this sweet dog. He has progressed slowly but steadily. Every week we notice something he is doing differently. We moved the kennel cage from the dining room to the laundry room after the first nine months. I thought he would like that better—just a little more privacy for his escape.

I was wrong. He returned to just staying in the corner, so I removed his bed from the kennel cage and put it in the corner for him. I was surprised when, after a week, he quit lying in the kennel bed and started finding other areas in the living room he liked to lie in. This was a very good sign that he was feeling comfortable enough in the house to pick several sleeping areas.

For the past couple of weeks, he has picked our bedroom to sleep at night. When he first started to go into our room, he did not want me to see that he was there. He would hide around the corner of the bed until I got into bed, and then he would come to lie on the floor by me. He has always picked my side of the room to stay on. A month ago I moved his bed into our room in front of the fireplace, and he now sleeps in it every night. The best part is that he doesn't care if I see him now.

The next thing he changed was his coming almost into the room we were in during the evening. A few weeks ago he started peeking into the living room at us and then lying in the doorway. Step by step, he has come closer to us. Now I am very pleased to say that after two years he will not only come all the way into the room, but he will lie on a throw blanket on the floor by the couch we are sitting on.

About a month ago he started jumping up on the couch if we were not in the room. If we entered, he would jump down and lie on the floor. Last week he started staying on the couch and only moving if we sat down. Now he will stay, but only if we sit at the other end of the couch. Remember that it has taken two years to get this little dog to feel safe enough to let this happen. I see this as a huge accomplishment for both of us.

There are times when he will walk up to us and touch his nose to our leg or hand if we are sitting. He sits by me when I eat, and he will take food offered by hand at the end of our meal. I am aware that many animal owners will cringe upon hearing that I offer him table food. I offer only a piece of the meat, and I have used this to build a relationship. He has not gained weight, and the offering is small.

Grooming is still very traumatizing to him. Only on the last appointment did he walk through the store to the grooming area without doing a nervous dump on the floor. He rides in the car quite well to his appointments, be they vet or grooming, but he is still nervous.

Valentino

Dog Information			
Name	Valentino	Sex	Neutered Male
Breed	Bichon	Color	White
Age/DOB	3 year	Hair	Cut Short

Markings/ Distinguishing Characteristics

March 27, 2014

We had a very sad Memorial weekend. On Friday morning Chase was not acting like himself. He did not eat his breakfast, and I did not like his breathing pattern. It was too heavy and deep. Being a respiratory therapist, I notice breathing. I pointed it out to Dale, who would only be working a half day. He would contact the vet, if needed, when he got home.

When Dale got home, Chase was dead. Valentino would not leave his side, which made it difficult for Dale to pick up Chase and remove him from the inside garage kennel. We are not taking Chase's death well, but Valentino is very much in depression. He has reverted back to being alone. He does not play, and his fluffy tail is not curled up on his back but is tucked down between his legs.

We can only hope that his mourning will not take away the progress we have made in helping him feel secure. He has not stopped eating, and he doesn't withdraw back into his kennel, but he has such a sad look to him, and he doesn't show any sign that he wants to run and play any longer. I think only time will help his and our broken hearts.

April 21, 2014

Looking for ways to help Valentino get past losing Chase, and because he likes Mr. Boots, I brought in a kitten that has been hanging around the house. I had been calling it Runt, but after taking it to the vet for shots and to set the appointment to have it neutered, I was told it is a girl. Her name is Renee now.

Valentino does not seem to care about her one bit. I tried, but Renee is just not the same as his friend.

June 7, 2014

Dale decided he could no longer handle the depression Valentino was in. It was time to get a puppy.

We picked up Mouser, a French Brittany Dale found on the Internet. He is very cute but full of energy that Valentino does not seem to want to keep up with yet. We had hoped Valentino would want to play again, but he just watches this puppy jump and play without joining in. This is going to be interesting.

We have a large kennel cage for Mouser to sleep in at night, and I was surprised to see Valentino join him. I knew Valentino seemed to like a kennel, and at times he had gone into one if company came over, as if it was his safe place. I don't feel that his returning to a kennel is a step backward. It's just an option he can use or not. We are hoping that his joining Mouser in the kennel is his acceptance of the puppy and a step forward.

July 6, 2014

The boys have been getting along great. Today they were cuddled together, sleeping in a chair on the deck at the cottage. It was very cute. They have a game they play at home: running around the deck together and jumping in each other's face, barking, and then running some more. I think getting Valentino another playmate was the best thing we could have done for him at this point. He no longer runs to the outside kennel as if he's looking for Chase when we return from the cottage.

August 20, 2014

Valentino has an ear infection. Rhonda found it at his grooming appointment last Saturday. He was not happy to go to the vet.

Now he has medication to put in his ear. This scares him so bad that he poops each time I pick him up to apply the medication. I will be glad when this is over. I am tired of chasing him around the room as he drops little bombs every few feet.

When I took him to the vet, we had some time in the room before the vet came in. I took the time to talk to him, rubbing his back and ears the entire time. He did not seem to mind it, but he still turned his head away if I tried to look him in the face. I don't know if that will ever change. I took a few pictures because he is so cute. I bet he does not know how much I love him.

October 16, 2014

Valentino now gets on the couch when we are in the room with him. Tonight I sat at the opposite end of the couch from where he was, and he did not get down and leave the room, so I pushed the boundary a little. I lay down on the couch, putting my feet by him and my head at the other end. He did not move! Only a couple of months short of three years, and this sweet dog will allow me to lie near him. I think he really does like me!

November 3, 2014

Since we have a horse ranch, we have stray cats that show up every now and then. At times we find litters of kittens in the barn or around the ranch, and we have no idea where they came from. I do believe some people think that if someone else lives in the country and has a barn, they have the right to drop off cats there.

We are having a cold November this year. Michigan can get that way. This morning Dale went to take care of the horses and found three kittens on our porch. He thought they were dead.

I went to see them and found one that was alive. I brought it in and warmed a dishcloth in the microwave to heat it. It took four times of trying to get the kitten to drink before I could get it to swallow. I have named it Rocky because it looks like a baby raccoon and is having a rocky start in life. Valentino just kind of sniffs at her, but that is all the interest he has.

January 5, 2015

We went through the holidays with Valentino not hiding from guests this year. He didn't interact with anyone; he just wanted to observe what was going on. If anyone went to him, he walked away. Every change in his openness to others in the home gives me the feeling of a proud parent watching her child conquer his fears and learn something new.

Sometimes he will lie in the sun coming through the patio doors, rolled onto his back, his little legs up in the air. I take this as a sign that he is very comfortable in our home. He trusts that he can sleep anywhere in our home and that he is safe. I may be reading more into this than I should, but seeing him behave as a normal pet after the fear he showed in the beginning is very comforting to me.

June 20, 2015

Valentino will now lie next to us on the couch. He still does not like to be touched, and he will move if we show him too much attention. I know Valentino will never be a "lap dog" wanting to be cuddled or scratched behind his ears. He does not like company coming over, but he seems to be fine after they are there for a while. People will go to him, wanting to pet him, but he wants nothing to do with being touched.

He is relaxed at home with Dale and me, and he has even licked my hand, which is something I did not expect. The little kisses dogs give are often taken for granted by owners. With Valentino, it was a milestone.

December 4, 2015

We did it again. We were in a pet store, looking for a dog for our daughter. This dog would not live with us, but will visit with our daughter at times. We sent her pictures and gave her the information on this cute little Yorkie Silky mix. She said she wanted it, but once we purchased the dog for her, she changed her mind. Even though we could return the dog and get most of the money back, everyone in our house—Valentino, Mouser, Mr. Boots, Renee, Rocky, Dale, and I—fell in love with her.

Her name is Hannah. She is small like Valentino, only thirteen pounds, and she is the sweetest little thing with her pink bow in her hair. Valentino seems to think she is his special Christmas gift. Mouser does not seem to care if she's around or not, but Valentino is in love. He follows her around and wants to lie down wherever she is sleeping. I think this is a better match for companionship than Mouser. Who knew that all he needed was a little girl the same size as him? Chase was so much bigger than he is, and Mouser, also being a Brittany, is much bigger. Or maybe it isn't the size. It may be because she's a female.

January 4, 2016

I don't believe we will be taking on new pets again soon. We have a houseful with three dogs and three cats. Dale and I do not have boring evenings. Mouser's antics are still evidence of "puppy mode"; Hannah follows us everywhere; and the cats play with anything they can bat around. Valentino now behaves like a dog who is very comfortable in his home. It has been a long road to get him there, only one month short of three years.

I hear about people getting pets for Christmas, or at other gift times, and then getting rid of them shortly afterward. Taking an animal into a new home can be traumatic for the animal. It is not unusual for the animal to show signs of not being housebroken, to chew on things other than their toys, or to not be the loveable animals people expect when they adopt them. You have to give an animal time to settle into a new world.

If the animal was a rescue, there is a history you probably know nothing about. Often that history is not good. The animal may have fears you don't see. Not all dogs shake and crouch next to a wall for safety like Valentino did, but that doesn't mean they aren't afraid. A pet needs to explore his new home, realize boundaries, and feel safe.

In writing this, I wanted to show people who are looking to bring pets, especially rescued animals into their homes that this can be challenging, particularly if they are looking for instant acceptance from the animals and the benefits the animals can bring to their homes. It takes time, patience, and understanding. The animal's love comes afterward. And in the case of Valentino, it was well worth the wait.

About the Author

Vicky L. Flora lives in Merrill, Michigan, with husband Dale, three horses, three cats, and three dogs. They have six children and nine grandchildren.

Vicky holds a Bachelor of Science degree in respiratory care from Independence University, Salt Lake City, Utah. She also has an associate's degree in respiratory care and an associate's degree in humanities from Delta College, University Center, Michigan. She is registered nationally as an asthma educator, holding the credentials of AE-C.

References

Weil, M. 1981. *Bichon Frise*.

Printed in the United States
By Bookmasters